A CENTURY *of*
HULL

The premises of J. Gohl, Wholesale Confectioner at 73 Queen Street, are even more impressive than usual in this picture since the shop is festooned with decorations to mark the coronation of George V in 1911. Among the goods on offer are toffees at 4d per pound.

A CENTURY *of* HULL

DAVID GERRARD

This book was first published in 2000 by Sutton Publishing

This new paperback edition first published in 2007 by Sutton Publishing

Reprinted in 2009 by
The History Press
The Mill, Brimscombe Port,
Stroud, Gloucestershire, GL5 2QG
www.thehistorypress.co.uk

British Library Cataloguing in Publication Data
A catalogue record for this book is available from the British Library.

ISBN 978 0 7509 4894 4

Front endpaper: Corporation dustcart, c. 1905.
Back endpaper: Victoria Pier, early twentieth century.
Half title page: A sturdy old barge steams into the Albert Dock, c. 1900.
Title page: Holy Trinity Church, c. 1900.

Typeset in 11/14pt Photina.
Typesetting and origination by
Sutton Publishing.
Printed and bound in England by
Athenaeum Press Ltd.

St Andrew's Dock in a period of prosperity, 1950s.

Contents

A busy scene in the Market Place, c. 1900, with St Mary's Church, Lowgate, in the distance. What looks at first sight like a large wall hanging, about halfway along the shops on the right, is actually a huge display of wicker baskets.

Britain: A Century of Change

Two women encumbered with gas masks go about their daily tasks during the early days of the war. (Hulton Getty Picture Collection)

T he sixty years ending in 1900 were a period of huge trans-
formation for Britain. Railway stations, post-and-telegraph offices,
police and fire stations, gasworks and gasometers, new livestock
markets and covered markets, schools, churches, football grounds,
hospitals and asylums, water pumping stations and sewerage plants
totally altered the urban scene, and the country's population tripled
with more than seven out of ten people being born in or moving to the
towns. The century that followed, leading up to the Millennium's end in
2000, was to be a period of even greater change.

When Queen Victoria died in 1901, she was measured for her
coffin by her grandson Kaiser Wilhelm, the London prostitutes put on
black mourning and the blinds came down in the villas and terraces
spreading out from the old town centres. These centres were reachable
by train and tram, by the new bicycles and still newer motor cars,
were connected by the new telephone, and lit by gas or even electricity.
The shops may have been full of British-made cotton and woollen
clothing but the grocers and butchers were selling cheap Danish bacon,
Argentinian beef, Australasian mutton and tinned or dried fish and fruit
from Canada, California and South Africa. Most of these goods were
carried in British-built-and-crewed ships burning Welsh steam coal.

As the first decade moved on, the Open Spaces Act meant more parks,
bowling greens and cricket pitches. The First World War transformed
the place of women, as they took over many men's jobs. Its other
legacies were the war memorials which joined the statues of Victorian
worthies in main squares round the land. After 1918 death duties and
higher taxation bit hard, and a quarter of England changed hands in
the space of only a few years.

The multiple shop – the chain store – appeared in the high street:
Sainsburys, Maypole, Lipton's, Home & Colonial, the Fifty Shilling Tailor,
Burton, Boots, W.H. Smith. The shopper was spoilt for choice, attracted
by the brash fascias and advertising hoardings for national brands like
Bovril, Pears Soap, and Ovaltine. Many new buildings began to be seen,
such as garages, motor showrooms, picture palaces (cinemas), 'palais
de dance', and ribbons of 'semis' stretched along the roads and new
bypasses and onto the new estates nudging the green belts.

During the 1920s cars became more reliable and sophisticated as well
as commonplace, with developments like the electric self-starter making
them easier for women to drive. Who wanted to turn a crank handle
in the new short skirt? This was, indeed, the electric age as much as
the motor era. Trolley buses, electric trams and trains extended mass
transport and electric light replaced gas in the street and the home,
which itself was groomed by the vacuum cleaner.

A major jolt to the march onward and upward was administered by
the Great Depression of the early 1930s. The older British industries

– textiles, shipbuilding, iron, steel, coal – were already under pressure from foreign competition when this worldwide slump arrived. Luckily there were new diversions to alleviate the misery. The 'talkies' arrived in the cinemas; more and more radios and gramophones were to be found in people's homes; there were new women's magazines, with fashion, cookery tips and problem pages; football pools; the flying feats of women pilots like Amy Johnson; the Loch Ness Monster; cheap chocolate and the drama of Edward VIII's abdication.

Things were looking up again by 1936 and new light industry was booming in the Home Counties as factories struggled to keep up with the demand for radios, radiograms, cars and electronic goods, including the first television sets. The threat from Hitler's Germany meant rearmament, particularly of the airforce, which stimulated aircraft and aero engine firms. If you were lucky and lived in the south, there was good money to be earned. A semi-detached house cost £450, a Morris Cowley £150. People may have smoked like chimneys but life expectancy, since 1918, was up by 15 years while the birth rate had almost halved.

In some ways it is the little memories that seem to linger longest from the Second World War: the kerbs painted white to show up in

A W.H.Smith shop front in Beaconsfield, 1922.

the blackout, the rattle of ack-ack shrapnel on roof tiles, sparrows killed by bomb blast. The biggest damage, apart from London, was in the south-west (Plymouth, Bristol) and the Midlands (Coventry, Birmingham). Postwar reconstruction was rooted in the Beveridge Report which set out the expectations for the Welfare State. This, together with the nationalisation of the Bank of England, coal, gas, electricity and the railways, formed the programme of the Labour government in 1945.

Times were hard in the late 1940s, with rationing even more stringent than during the war. Yet this was, as has been said, 'an innocent and well-behaved era'. The first let-up came in 1951 with the Festival of Britain and there was another fillip in 1953 from the Coronation, which incidentally gave a huge boost to the spread of TV. By 1954 leisure motoring had been resumed but the Comet – Britain's best hope for taking on the American aviation industry – suffered a series of mysterious crashes. The Suez debacle of 1956 was followed by an acceleration in the withdrawal from Empire, which had begun in 1947 with the Independence of India. Consumerism was truly born with the advent of commercial TV and most homes soon boasted washing machines, fridges, electric irons and fires.

Children collecting aluminium to help the war effort, London, 1940s. (IWM)

A street party to celebrate the Queen's Coronation, June 1953. (Hulton Getty Picture Collection)

The Lady Chatterley obscenity trial in 1960 was something of a straw in the wind for what was to follow in that decade. A collective loss of inhibition seemed to sweep the land, as the Beatles and the Rolling Stones transformed popular music, and retailing, cinema and the theatre were revolutionised. Designers, hairdressers, photographers and models moved into places vacated by an Establishment put to flight by the new breed of satirists spawned by Beyond the Fringe and Private Eye.

In the 1970s Britain seems to have suffered a prolonged hangover after the excesses of the previous decade. Ulster, inflation and union troubles were not made up for by entry into the EEC, North Sea Oil, Women's Lib or, indeed, Punk Rock. Mrs Thatcher applied the corrective in the 1980s, as the country moved more and more from its old manufacturing base over to providing services, consulting, advertising, and expertise in the 'invisible' market of high finance or in IT.

The post-1945 townscape has seen changes to match those in the worlds of work, entertainment and politics. In 1952 the Clean Air Act served notice on smogs and pea-souper fogs, smuts and blackened buildings, forcing people to stop burning coal and go over to smokeless sources of heat and energy. In the same decade some of the best urban building took place in the 'new towns' like Basildon, Crawley, Stevenage and Harlow. Elsewhere open warfare was declared on slums and what was labelled inadequate, cramped, back-to-back, two-up, two-down, housing. The new 'machine for living in' was a flat in a high-rise block. The architects and planners who promoted these

Punk rockers demonstrate their anarchic style during the 1970s. (Barnaby's Picture Library)

were in league with the traffic engineers, determined to keep the motor car moving whatever the price in multi-storey car parks, meters, traffic wardens and ring roads. The old pollutant, coal smoke, was replaced by petrol and diesel exhaust, and traffic noise.

Fast food was no longer only a pork pie in a pub or fish-and-chips. There were Indian curry houses, Chinese take-aways and American-style hamburgers, while the drinker could get away from beer in a wine bar. Under the impact of television the big Gaumonts and Odeons closed or were rebuilt as multi-screen cinemas, while the palais de dance gave way to discos and clubs.

From the late 1960s the introduction of listed buildings and conservation areas, together with the growth of preservation societies, put a brake on 'comprehensive redevelopment'. The end of the century and the start of the Third Millennium see new challenges to the health of towns and the wellbeing of the nine out of ten people who now live urban lives. The fight is on to prevent town centres from dying, as patterns of housing and shopping change, and edge-of-town supermarkets exercise the attractions of one-stop shopping. But as banks and department stores close, following the haberdashers, greengrocers,

Millennium celebrations over the Thames at Westminster. New Year's Eve, 1999. (Barnaby's Picture Library)

butchers and ironmongers, there are signs of new growth such as farmers' markets, and corner stores acting as pick-up points where customers collect shopping ordered on-line from web sites.

Futurologists tell us that we are in stage two of the consumer revolution: a shift from mass consumption to mass customisation driven by a desire to have things that fit us and our particular lifestyle exactly, and for better service. This must offer hope for small city-centre shop premises, as must the continued attraction of physical shopping, browsing and being part of a crowd: in a word, 'shoppertainment'. Another hopeful trend for towns is the growth in the number of young people postponing marriage and looking to live independently, alone, where there is a buzz, in 'swinging single cities'. Their's is a 'flats-and-cafés' lifestyle, in contrast to the 'family suburbs', and certainly fits in with government's aim of building 60 per cent of the huge amount of new housing needed on 'brown' sites, recycled urban land. There looks to be plenty of life in the British town yet.

Hull: An Introduction

The City of Hull began the twentieth century as a prosperous, vibrant and self-confident community. This was again true at the end of the century, but in between these high points the city's fortunes fluctuated wildly. As well as enduring, along with rest of the country, two world wars and the Great Depression of the 1920s and '30s, the city was also vulnerable to the vagaries of maritime trade, its economic life-blood. The collapse of the fishing industry in the '70s was perhaps the city's lowest point, affecting as it did almost every family in the city. But in the last quarter of the century, Hull has picked itself up, dusted itself down, and recovered the optimism and assurance of a hundred years earlier.

Hull entered the century proudly, having been created a city just three years earlier, in Queen Victoria's Diamond Jubilee year. Its population then was around 240,000, a figure which has increased remarkably little, only rising to around 265,000 in 1996. The great majority of the city's workforce in 1900 was employed either in the great fishing fleet or on the docks which extended for some 10 miles alongside the Humber and the Hull. Two major docks had been constructed in the 1880s, St Andrew's and Alexandra, and a third, the King George Dock, opened in 1914.

Four years into the century, Hull's unique municipal telephone service opened in a converted public bathhouse. The system covered an area of 120 square miles and its switchboard, attended by 20 female operators, had a maximum capacity of serving 2,000 subscribers. By the end of the century, Kingston Telecommunications, as it had now become, had 170,000 customers and the company's flotation in 1999 brought a substantial windfall to the City Treasury.

In the same year that Hull's telephone system began operating, the city and the country were appalled by what became known as the 'Russian Outrage'. On 22 October 1904, the Russian Baltic squadron opened fire on some fifty Hull trawlers fishing near the Dogger Bank. The Russian commander said he thought the trawlers were part of the Japanese fleet. (Tsarist Russia was then at war with Japan.) Two fishermen were killed in the attack and a third died later from his wounds.

The beginning of the second decade of the century was marked by a generous donation to the city, in 1911, of about 50 acres of land to be developed into a public park. The benefactor was the wealthy ship-owner Christopher Pickering from whom the park takes its name.

Three years later, the office of Mayor of Hull was elevated to the dignity of Lord Mayor. He retained his additional title of Admiral of the Humber, which dates back to a charter of Henry VI granted in 1447 which entrusted the Corporation to appoint a 'suitable and discreet man'. Within the Humber area he took precedence over all Admirals of England. These powers later lapsed but the City's Lord Mayor is still, ex officio, Admiral of the Humber during his year of office and the captains of naval ships, British or foreign, on courtesy visits to the port, always call on the Admiral at the Guildhall and subsequently receive him or her aboard their vessels.

The Guildhall, a stately Edwardian building which is still the headquarters of the City Council, was completed in 1914. And in June of that year, George V visited the city to open the King George Dock. The dock didn't actually start operating until 25 August 1914 – three days before the start of the First World War.

When war was declared, some 20,000 Hull men and women volunteered to serve in the Armed Forces – an astonishing number, representing almost 1 in 12 of the population. Seven thousand of them lost their lives. The War Office requisitioned 300 Hull-registered ships: only 91 of them returned to their home port. (In contrast, 1,200 people were killed during the Second World War despite nine months of heavy bombing raids.)

An interesting mix of vehicles on Anlaby Road, 1930s. They range from the horse and cart on the left, through the 'Art Dyers' delivery van and a stately trolley bus, to the sporty model in the foreground.

In 1915, the city suffered several air raids by Zeppelins. One of them, in June of that year, left 24 dead, and 40 shops and houses destroyed. German submarines put a stop to fishing in the North Sea and even when the war finally ended, the fishing industry's recovery was slow.

An atmospheric shot of the old Monument Bridge. c. 1904.

The 1920s saw the foundation of Hull's University College by Thomas Ferens, who also bequeathed a substantial sum to build the Ferens Art Gallery which opened in 1927. But the decade opened with a major disaster, the loss of the R38 airship over the River Humber. The great ship was on its last trial flight before being delivered to the US Navy. As it turned sharply over the river, the R38 broke in two, exploded into flames and crashed into the river. In the cemetery near West Park is a memorial to the 44 men who lost their lives in the tragedy.

Aviation produced a much happier story in the 1930s when the city took great pride in the exploits of its most famous daughter, Amy Johnson, the first woman pilot to fly solo from England to Australia.

This decade also saw the creation of one of the city's most attractive amenities. Thousands of tons of rubble were dumped into the redundant eighteenth-century Queen's Dock. Atop the garbage, Queen's Gardens was developed – now one of the most attractive city centre parks in Britain. At the same time, the lofty, 150ft high Wilberforce Monument was moved to a new site at the northern end of the gardens.

The Second World War inflicted terrible damage on the city, as shown later in this book. Herbert Morrison, a senior member of the War Cabinet, later voiced his opinion that of all the major British cities, Hull had suffered most.

Hull's regeneration after the war was slow in coming. A boom in the fishing industry in the late 1940s and early '50s revitalised the city's economy for a while but 1958 saw the inception of the Cod War which was to have such disastrous implications for the city. In that year Iceland declared a 12-mile limit for fishing off its shores. Previously, British trawlers could fish the North Atlantic waters up to 4 miles from the Icelandic coast. To begin with, the ban was largely ignored but the dispute with Iceland was to flare up again, disastrously, some 15 years later.

A striking view of the city from the air. The large building in the centre is the Guildhall and post office. Note the impressive collection of barges huddled along the bank of the River Hull.

The 1960s saw an orgy of redevelopment across the city, most of it brutally ugly. But a surprising number of elegant Victorian and Edwardian buildings had escaped the Luftwaffe's bombs. They stand out all the better among the characterless structures of the 1960s surrounding them.

The 1970s could well be called Hull's 'Dreadful Decade'. In 1972, Iceland raised the stakes in the Cod War by extending the fishing limit for foreign trawlers to 100 miles from its coast. Ships ignoring the ban were fired on and the conflict peaked when two British trawlers were sunk by Icelandic gunboats in September 1972. Britain's eventual acceptance of the Icelandic ban led ineluctably to the demise of Hull's once famously prosperous fishing fleet.

In contrast, the 1980s was a period of returning self-confidence. The awe-inspiring Humber Bridge opened in 1981 and the introduction of the Northern Ferries roll-on/roll-off ferries generated a rapid expansion of freight and passenger traffic from Hull to Rotterdam and Zeebrugge. Hull is still the largest timber port in the UK and also handles vast quantities of grain, oilseeds and wool. Altogether, cargoes of more than 10 million tonnes pass through the port each year and the ferries carry more than a million passengers each year.

In 1980, the Tidal Surge Barrier across the mouth of the River Hull was completed, protecting the Old Town from the frequent flooding it had endured over the years. And in 1983, the former Humber Dock was converted into the Hull Marina.

The final decade of the century saw the Prince's Quay Shopping Centre created atop 500 stilts in the old Prince's Dock. With its 70 shops on four floors and its pleasant waterside setting, the Centre has become one of the major shopping venues in the north-east. To the west of the city, St Andrew's Dock was converted into a leisure park, complete with multi-screen cinema, restaurants and a riverside promenade.

Unlike the 1960s developments, these projects are all well-designed and display an imaginative and sympathetic use of the Humber waterfront and the old docks. As in 1900, the city is once again a great port, a great city and a great place to live.

The Start of the Century

This gleaming, gilded sculpture of William III in Hull's Market Place is one of the most impressive equestrian statues in Britain. Hull was the first major city to declare its allegiance to William of Orange in the Glorious Revolution of 1685 which deposed James II. This magnificent statue by the Dutch sculptor Peter Scheemaker showing his compatriot garbed as a Roman emperor was erected in 1734, funded by a public subscription at a cost of 785 guineas. The gilding was added in 1768 and has been frequently renewed over the years.

The creators of this unusual postcard were making a satirical comment on the slow progress of constructing the new Monument Bridge in 1906. Their card guaranteed free access to view the progress of the work, which they apparently expected to continue until January 2006. It also mocks the North Eastern Railway, suggesting that its initials, NER, stood for 'Never Expect Rapidity'.

A fine view of Prince's Dock with the Wilberforce Memorial in the centre and the triple-towered Docks Office in the background. When Prince's Dock was completed in 1829 it transformed the old part of the city into an island. Originally unnamed, it was christened Prince's Dock after the visit of Queen Victoria and Prince Albert in 1854.

The grand building dominating the Market Place is Holy Trinity Church. It is the largest English parish church in terms of floor area and is believed to be the oldest brick building in England still in use for its original purpose. The central tower dates from about 1500; the splendid nave with its 8 bays from around 1400; and the oldest parts, the chancel and transepts, are early fourteenth century.

Another view of the church reveals a curious circular building with a filigreed dome on the left of the picture. This was a public urinal. Such conveniences, pissoirs, were a commonplace on the Continent at the time but this one may well have been unique in England. Sadly, it was demolished in the 1920s.

A travelling fruit, flower and vegetable vendor and his family outside Woodhouse Place. They seem to be offering a fairly meagre range of goods and the windows of 'J. Major, Practical Boot Maker' behind them also display a minimal range of footwear on sale.

On the quay of St Andrew's Dock, early 1900s. The aproned women were the 'fisher girls', noted for their dexterity at 'gipping' – skinning, gutting and filleting the fish. About 60 herring a minute was the average but some girls could dispose of up to 100 in the same time.

A crowded paddle-steamer ferry boat, the Humber, at Spurn Point, c. 1910, a time when passengers were not provided with protection from the weather. The ferry boats were occasionally used for excursions round Spurn Point to Withernsea, but the presence of a naval officer and rating in the smaller boat suggest that this may have been a sea burial.

A busy scene at Victoria Pier, c. 1905. This was the departure point for ferries across the Humber, a service which had been in regular operation since at least the 1300s. Scheduled services to New Holland on the south bank (a 2½ mile journey at this point), began in 1820 and continued until the opening of the Humber Bridge in 1981.

Alexandra Dock was built by the Hull and Barnsley Railway and when it opened in 1885 was the largest on the east coast. Although it was closed for 9 years during the 1980s it is now operating again. The dock has been accorded a Grade I listing as a structure worthy of conservation and even some of its machinery, such as a 100-ton steam crane of 1886, has earned Grade II status.

An impressive group of city notables, led by the Lord Mayor, Alderman Larard, gathered to inaugurate Hull's first tram service in 1899. During the first six months of operation more than 4 million passengers travelled on these stately vehicles.

Two photographers have set up their tripods in the roadway to record the grand procession following the inaugural drive. In its heyday between the wars, the Hull tramway system extended over 27 miles of permanent way, serviced by a fleet of 150 cars.

This precarious-looking contraption passing down King Edward Street was known as the 'Electric Tram Car Wire Rully'. From its platform, the workmen could service and repair the overhead wires.

Positive identification of this couple and their splendid automobile has not been possible but it's believed that they were members of the Reckitt family. This prosperous manufacturing family, whose world-famous products included starch and 'Reckitt's Blue' (actually a whitener used in laundering), were keen motorists from the very earliest days.

A popular short excursion from Hull was to the windmill at Hessle which was used to grind chalk from the nearby quarry. It was built in 1810 and, although no longer working, it's still there – dwarfed nowadays by the north tower of the Humber Bridge in whose shadow it stands. The older lady in the photograph has been identified as Mrs Susannah Nicholson Smith, a former Lady Mayoress of Doncaster; the younger lady is her daughter, Susie Nicholson Holmes.

Great excitement was caused, it appears, by the visit of the Postmaster-General on 22 July 1909. He had come to officially open the new General Post Office, a grand building described as being 'constructed in a monumental Renaissance style similar to the Paris Opera'.

King Edward Street was created at the turn of the nineteenth century when old, insanitary housing was cleared and replaced by commercial retail outlets. The sandwich-board man on the right is advertising for H. Samuel's store in Silver Street – 'The largest sale in the world of Silverware, Cruets & Cutlery'. It's difficult to understand why the group of bystanders, bottom right, has been so crudely drawn in.

A splendid old locomotive chugs into Hedon station on the Hull to Withernsea line. During the first half of the century this line was popular with summer holidaymakers on their way to the east coast resort. The service fell victim to the Beeching cuts in the 1960s but much of the trackbed has survived and is now a cycle route.

A motley group of desperate-looking men monopolise a bench outside the Kingston Street headquarters of the Manchester, Sheffield and Lincolnshire Railway, c. 1905. Despite the building's impressive frontage no passenger trains ran from here, only freight services. And where the MSL did provide passenger trains, its reputation for customer care was abysmal. Its initials were generally interpreted as standing for 'Mucky, Slow and Lazy'.

27

When this photograph was taken in about 1908, Paragon station was one of five stations in the city. Today, it's the only one. Built in 1847, this elegant and functional building was replaced by a brutally functional and completely inelegant frontage in the 1960s. The memorial statue, bottom centre, commemorated the men of Hull who lost their lives in the Boer Wars. To the left of the picture is the Royal Station Hotel where Queen Victoria lodged during her visit to Hull in 1854.

Another impressive nineteenth-century building. It's not a baronial castle but Hull Gaol on Hedon Road, built in 1869 and still in use. The gaol respected a civic tradition stretching back to Georgian times that all public buildings, however grim their purpose, should display some architectural merit. Even workhouses, built to house the most socially disadvantaged, often mimicked stately homes. The living conditions inside both kinds of institutions were a different matter.

An organ grinder and his family wait near Victoria Pier to entertain the next ferry load of passengers. An Italian by origin, the organ grinder was a familiar sight for many years, together with his wife who, as here, was always dressed in a crisp white apron. A small monkey was also part of the show but is not visible here.

Paragon Street, early 1900s. The impressive Theatre Royal, on the right, had been built in 1871 with seating for up to 1,200. It provided a major venue for touring companies for many years until incompetent management led to its closure in 1909. The theatre then stood empty for 3 years before re-opening as the Tivoli Palace of Varieties. One of the many popular acts to perform at the new Tivoli was The Silent Humourist, a juggler by the name of W.C. Fields, in 1913. Two years later, a minor role in a Ziegfeld Follies revue kick-started the bulbous-nosed comedian's legendary film career.

The most accessible form of entertainment at this time was, of course, the pub. One hopes that all these children outside the White Hart Inn in Alfred Gelder Street weren't waiting for their dads to come out. The Temperance Movement derided these lavishly appointed pubs as 'gin palaces'. The White Hart was definitely one of them and, happily, still is. Despite the devastating damage inflicted during the Second World War, Hull still boasts a rich heritage of splendid Victorian and Edwardian pubs.

The entertainment here is completely free. Two policemen are among the onlookers gathered to observe two labourers mending an unidentified road. There is a pre-echo here of those observation windows provided by today's builders of major projects for curious passers-by. The magnificent machine in the background dates the photograph to the early 1900s.

Another formidable piece of early twentieth-century machinery – a state-of-the-art road roller makes easy work of levelling a road surface. The monster was steered by a chain attached to the driving wheel – part of the chain can be seen on the bottom right front corner of the machine.

In 1903, a Hull newspaper deplored the 'walking fever' that had gripped the nation. The writer mocked the 'grotesque style' of some of the competitors in walking races. Perhaps he had just witnessed this contest, organised by Hull grocers. Walking mania peaked in about 1904, its popularity waning as automobile traffic increased and the police decided to become more vigilant in arresting walkers for 'wilfully obstructing the free passage of the highway'.

No such public order problems arose at this peaceful cricket match at Hymers College, c. 1908. The school, opened in 1893 by the Revd John Hymers, stands in 30 acres of beautiful grounds on the edge of West Park. At that time the school was for boys only but it now also admits girls.

Hull is particularly well provided with public parks and gardens. This charming scene was photographed at the drinking water fountain in Pearson Park, whose 27 acres were donated to the town in 1860 by Zachariah Pearson, Mayor of Hull in that year. Pearson had made his fortune as a prudent shipowner, but lost everything when he badly miscalculated the risks of trying to evade the blockade imposed by the Americans during their Civil War of 1861–5.

Pickering Park, opened on 13 July 1911, was another donation to the city – in this case by the businessman Christopher Pickering, co-founder in 1885 of the highly successful Pickering & Haldane's Steam Trawling Co. Special features of the park included a sizeable boating lake and a bandstand.

The Newland Sailors Orphans Home was founded in 1853. Safety standards for sailors on ships of that time, and until well into the twentieth century, ensured a steady stream of applicants for entry to the Home. The 29 children in this photograph, taken in about 1909, had all lost their fathers; the austere rules of the Home ensured that their impoverished mothers would find it almost impossible to maintain any kind of meaningful relationship with their sons.

The provision of school supplies at the School Order Dept of A. Brown & Sons, Savile Street, was obviously taken very seriously since three of its clerks appear to be fully occupied in servicing a single order. The company is still in existence, today occupying premises on George Street.

Street urchins in Green Lane, 1907. In that year, Sir James Reckitt wrote to the shipowner Thomas Ferens: 'Whilst I and my family live in beautiful houses, surrounded by lovely gardens and fine scenery, the work people we employ are, many of them, living in squalor'. Reckitt, a Quaker, became the leading figure among a group of Hull businessmen who pledged serious amounts of money to create a new Garden Village to the west of the city.

Sir James Reckitt himself contributed £100,000 to the Garden Village which was built between 1907 and 1909. The spacious, well-laid-out village included 600 homes, each provided with all the latest amenities. The village was considered such a credit to the city that official visitors to Hull were always invited to a conducted tour.

A crew member demonstrates the damage inflicted on his trawler, the St Moulmein, during the 'Russian Outrage' of 1904, an incident which incensed public opinion across the country. On the night of 22 October, some fifty Hull trawlers were fishing near the Dogger Bank when they were fired on without warning by ships of the Russian Baltic squadron. The Russians were then at war with Japan and the squadron commander later claimed that he had seen the flashing lights of the trawlers' acetylene lamps and believed that he was being attacked by the Japanese fleet. When the commander discovered his mistake, he made matters worse by sailing away without finding out whether the trawlermen needed assistance. In fact, two of the fishermen had been killed; a third died later from his wounds. An international commission was appointed to investigate the 'Dogger Bank Incident'. The Russian government eventually paid the trawlermen an indemnity of £65,000 – a very substantial sum but considerably less than the £103,830 the fishermen had claimed.

The three fishermen who had died in the 'Dogger Bank Incident' were buried with great pomp and ceremony as this impressive procession indicates. (The impressiveness is a little diminished by seeing that one of the three naval escorts alongside the first hearse, the middle one, seems to be seriously out of step.)

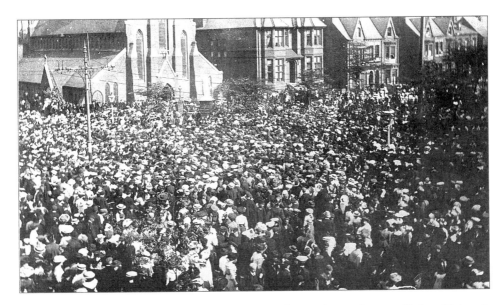

Three lives were lost in the 'Russian Outrage'. Ten thousand times that number assembled on 30 August 1906 to witness the unveiling of a memorial to the dead sailors. The statue of a gaberdine-clothed seaman was unveiled outside the Church of St Barnabas on The Boulevard and can just be seen near the centre top of the photograph. It still stands there.

The city was in a state of high excitement on 24 June 1914. On that day, King George V, accompanied by Queen Mary, arrived to open the newly built dock named after him. Although now officially opened, the dock was not actually ready for commercial operations until a month later, 25 July 1914. That was just three days before Britain became involved in the First World War. Within a few weeks, the War Office had requisitioned every seaworthy vessel in the port.

'Hull Brewery horses leaving the stables to render service for King & Country in the 1914–18 war.' Hundreds of thousands of horses were drafted from all across the country to provide transportation for an army which was still only minimally mechanised. Brewery horses were especially prized because of their immense strength, ideal for dragging artillery through the muddy wastes of Belgium. Few of them returned to peaceful pastures in England.

The after-effects of a Zeppelin air raid on Porter Street. The attack took place on 6 June 1915 and only occurred because strong headwinds had prevented the attacking airship reaching its intended target, London. Finding himself unexpectedly flying over Hull, another of Britain's most strategic ports, the commander of the Zeppelin decided to unleash his bombs. Twenty-four people were killed in this impromptu raid; 40 shops and houses were also destroyed.

Following the Armistice of 11 November 1918, every self-respecting street community held its own Peace Party. This one took place in Roberts Terrace, Marmaduke Street. A sing-song was clearly going to be part of the celebrations since an upright piano had been wheeled out into the street. It can just be discerned at the far end of the table.

Between the Wars

During the First World War, Prime Minister David Lloyd George promised that at the end of the conflict, the people of Britain would build 'a land fit for heroes'. In fact, the embryonic Welfare State was unable to cope with the problems posed by the large numbers of disabled war veterans and the unemployed. Many, like this itinerant street musician, endured a precarious existence dependent on charity.

In 1935, it was decided that Queen's Dock had outlived its usefulness. Thousands of tonnes of rubble were deposited in the dock and on top of this huge rubbish pit one of the city's most popular amenities was created – the present-day Queen's Gardens.

In the same year, the colossal Wilberforce Monument was moved from its site in the city centre to the eastern end of the Queen's Gardens. This literally 'monumental task' was carried out free of charge by a local building firm. The removal provided a rare opportunity to see the statue of the 'Great Emancipator' (ironically burdened here in heavy chains) close up. William was looking distinctly grubby after a century of exposure 150ft above the smoke from Hull's busy mills and factories.

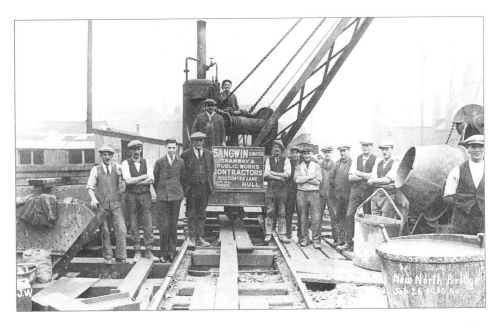

Construction in progress on the new North Bridge, 26 September 1930. It's interesting that many of the workforce of 'Sangwin Limited, Tramway & Public Works Contractors' apparently considered a 6-buttoned waistcoat, collar and tie to be suitable working apparel.

Construction on a more modest scale at Willoughby's Carpentry Shop. With mass production of do-it-yourself kits for almost any piece of furniture still well in the future, this was clearly a thriving enterprise.

43

Another successful family business was Mallory's General Store in Hessle Road. The comprehensive display of ironmongery on show here includes watering-cans from 2s 3d, and tin baths for 3s 5d. Between them, members of the Mallory family owned no fewer than 36 shops around the city. Their commercial success, however, did not ensure harmony among them. At any one time, various branches of the family would either not be on speaking terms or else communicating only through their lawyers.

Rudd's the Butchers in Hessle Road, Hull, puts on a grand presentation for its 'Xmas Show, 1931'. Mr Rudd, in the centre with his wife and young son, was clearly a patriotic man. There are 'Buy British' placards in among the dressed chickens and the board offers 'Good Sound Advice – Buy English & Have the Best'. The Rudd family owned four butcher's shops scattered across the city.

A sole policeman was considered adequate to keep the crowds under control as they waited for the opening of the Willis Bros autumn sale in 1938. The billboards offer a curious range of bargains: Fireplace Curbs for 6s 11d; '1000 Washing Dresses' for 2s, and 'Willow Tea Sets' for 3s 11d. The store was destroyed during an air raid in 1941 and the site on Carr Lane is now occupied by Allders store.

Mr and Mrs Ashton's mussels and whelks stall in Walton Street. The Ashtons were itinerant traders who followed the circuit of trade fairs, arriving here for the Hull Fair of 1933. Their daughter Muriel stands on the right of the picture. Behind them is the Asbestos Garages, a business whose name would be something of a deterrent to trade nowadays.

A sporty delivery vehicle in the service of J.J. Bradfield, Veal Purveyor. The registration number, AT 195, indicates that this motorised 3-wheeler was one of the earliest vehicles to have been registered in Hull. Note the klaxon on the left handlebar.

An interesting insight into how ice-cream was made in the 1930s. 'G. Portores for Quality Ices' says the advertising slogan on the banner leaning against the centre post. The ceiling appears to be colonised by growths of a dubious nature and hanging on the wall, upper right, is the bicycle with which Mr Portores transported his ice-creams around the city. He must have regretted agreeing to this picture being taken since the photographer was actually a City Health Inspector, and Mr Portores' business was subsequently closed down on health grounds.

'Registered Slaughterhouse No. 32, Coelus Street.' The Public Health Inspector's report was damning: 'Insanitary building. Killing and hanging [takes place] in one room. Insufficient light. Open to the public. Inadequate cleansing and draining facilities.' Not surprisingly, the slaughterhouse was closed down.

A barrel of whisky being removed from a bonded warehouse in Dagger Lane. (The lane, near the Market Place, has since disappeared under redevelopment.) The Customs and Excise official on the left would check the duty payable; the two police officers were in attendance to make sure that none of the liquor was illegally spirited away.

A misty morning view of the mixed fleet of drays and motor vehicles used by the Hull Brewery Co. The horse-drawn drays continued in operation until 1974. By then, the volume of city traffic had made it too dangerous for them to continue negotiating its streets and they were withdrawn.

A potentially dangerous incident on the Anlaby Road level crossing, 1936. The lorry, owned by 'Thomas West Ltd, Export Coopers', has broken down in the most inconvenient place possible. A curious detail in the photograph is the gatepost, bottom right, which carries an advertisement for 'Lighams Fountain Pen Ink'.

A solitary passenger waits for the 12.20pm to North Cave at Springhead Halt on the Hull & Barnsley railway, 1929. Although its freight trains produced a reasonable profit, passenger traffic on the line was never heavy and all passenger services were withdrawn in August 1955. The freight operations struggled on for a few more years but they too were terminated in 1961.

At Paragon station in October 1937 Brigadier General J.L.J. Clarke CMG, Colonel of the East Yorkshire Regiment, formally names the V2 locomotive, The Snapper. Known as the Green Arrow series, these London and North Eastern Railway locomotives were all named after British regiments. The East Yorkshire Regiment had earned the nickname of Snappers in the eighteenth century, a sobriquet which reflected its soldiers' terrier-like aggressiveness.

Contending with a stiff breeze and choppy water, the paddle-steamer ferry from Lincolnshire struggles to dock safely at the Victoria Pier.

Another precarious manoeuvre. Very occasionally, because of adverse weather, the ferry boats were unable to dock alongside the quay. Passengers were then conveyed by small boats from ferry to quay. It must have been quite a tricky business for this lady encumbered by the voluminous clothes of the time.

This vintage trawler, the Yorick, had an open bridge directly behind the funnel which made it very uncomfortable for the crew since they were often smothered in acrid smoke. The Yorick (length 111.43ft; breadth 24ft), was built at Beverley in 1909 as part of the 'Boxer Fleet'. These were smaller trawlers which would put their fish into boxes and then transfer them to a larger ship. The Yorick was finally scrapped in 1956.

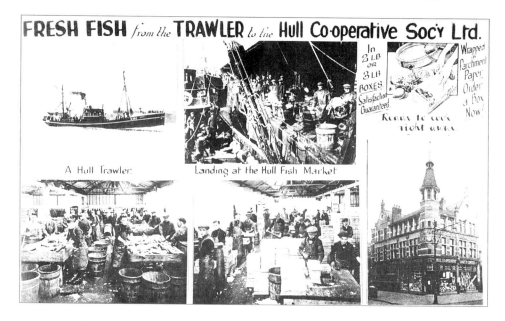

A promotional postcard produced by the Hull Co-operative Society tells the story of 'Fresh Fish from the Trawler' until it ended up at the Co-op's rather grand store on Jameson Street, where it was presented to the consumer hygienically 'Wrapped in Parchment Paper'.

A peaceful scene on the River Hull to the north of the city. The distinctive sail was known as a Norfolk Rig. The brickworks in the background have long since been demolished.

Considering this photograph was taken in the early 1920s, the clarity of such an early aerial view is remarkable. The impressive building centre left is the City Hall, which was completed in 1905. It faces Victoria Square and looks across to the triple-turreted Hull Docks Office. The broad thoroughfare running through the centre of the picture is Prospect Street with the Wilberforce Monument at its southern end.

Hull's most famous daughter, Amy Johnson, 'The Wonder Airwoman', was born in the city in 1903, gained her pilot's licence in 1929 and in the following year became the first woman to fly solo to Australia. Later, she made a record-breaking solo flight to Cape Town in 4½ days, taking 'a few books, maps, a bag full of iron rations and a pith helmet'. At the outbreak of the Second World War, Amy joined the Air Transport Auxiliary as a ferry pilot, but on 5 January 1941 she was lost after baling out over the Thames Estuary. A statue of the fearless aviatrix was erected in Prospect Street in 1976.

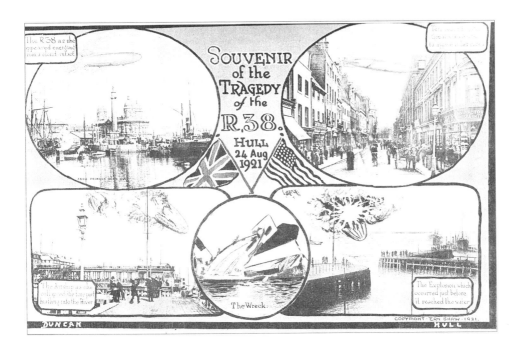

A postcard 'Souvenir of the Tragedy of the R38'. On 24 August 1921, the R38 was on its last trial flight before being handed over to the US Navy's flying wing. The Americans had already erected the biggest hangar in the world to house it at Lakehurst, New Jersey. The R38 airship was the largest yet built – 699ft long and carrying 2,700,000 cubic feet of hydrogen. On that August afternoon there were 49 people on board, among them 17 US Navy officers. At about 5pm the airship was flying over the Humber and turned sharply towards Hedon airfield. The manoeuvre broke the ship's back. Thousands of Hull citizens watched as the huge craft split in two and exploded into a fireball. The wreckage fell into the river near Victoria Pier and was still burning 24 hours later. Remarkably, there were 5 survivors, one of them the Captain.

The R38 tragedy halted airship production in Britain for several years, but in the late 1920s, the government decided to try once more and commissioned two new ships. One of them was the R100, seen here under construction at Hedon airfield in 1929. Designed by Barnes Wallis, the R100 was launched on 16 December 1929, and early the next year established an airship speed record of 81.5 mph.

A view from the passenger lounge looking forwards to the front section still under construction. Such is the scale of the airship that you have to look very hard to distinguish the riggers at work in the girder framework, top right. The R100 could accommodate 100 passengers and had a cruising range of 3,500 miles.

On its completion, visiting dignitaries were given a tour of the airship followed by complimentary high tea on the terrace balcony. The R100's flying career was to last less than a year. In October 1930, following the crash of its sister ship, the R101, in France with the loss of 48 lives, the airship building programme was abandoned. The R100 was dismantled and sold as scrap for £600.

The Graf Zeppelin LZ127 flying over King George Dock, 1936. These quiet and spacious Leviathans of the air were highly popular with transatlantic travellers in the 1920s and '30s. But when the Hindenburg, the world's largest airship, came down in flames in 1937, the brief age of the airship was over.

The 'toast-rack' style of travel, 1920s. These magnificent charabancs of the Grey Cars company are about to set off for an excursion from the Half Way Hotel on Hessle Road. The vehicles have long since gone to the wrecker's yard but the pub is still going strong.

Between the wars, patriotic spirit ensured that St George's Day was always celebrated with a colourful procession in which all the city's organisations took part. The main float carries the figures of a suitably plump 'John Bull' and an Amazonian-looking 'Britannia'.

Oak Farm Dairy's delivery carts stand festively decorated outside their Portland Street premises. It's not known which event they were taking part in, but it may well have been the same St George's Day parade seen above.

The years between the wars was a period when garden fêtes enjoyed their greatest popularity. Ducking for apples was an essential element of the entertainment. The houses in the background have been identified as Lee's Rest Homes, which pinpoints the location as Pickering Park.

Also guaranteed to create great merriment was the ladies' egg and spoon race. Typically, many of the ladies have kept their hats on, most of them rather fetching cloches.

A popular attraction in Pickering Park was the boating lake. Once again, the people in the boats have dutifully kept their hats on. The disappearance of headwear following the Second World War, after centuries during which it was regarded as obligatory, has been declared a fashion mystery.

A wonderfully atmospheric picture of barges on the River Hull, 1930s. Commercial traffic on Britain's canals and rivers was still important, with more than 9 million tonnes of freight being transported each year. Even today, barges still ply between Hull's Old Harbour, the Trent wharves and throughout the Aire & Calder canal system.

An environmentalist's dream of public transport. As the gates open on the Hessle Road level crossing, around 60 cyclists, 2 buses, 1 tram and a milk lorry prepare to surge ahead. Pollution level: virtually nil.

Costello Playing Fields, part of Anlaby Park and better known to local children as Peter Pan Park, 2 August 1932. Note the splendidly commodious perambulator and the boy in the centre with his model sailboat.

The year is 1937 and the Regal Cinema in Ferensway is showing Shirley Temple in Heidi. The cinema had been built just 3 years earlier, bringing the town's tally of cinemas to twenty-six. Most of them offered two completely different programmes each week and, in addition to the main feature, the programme would include a shorter 'B movie', one or more cartoons and a newsreel. At this time, Hull also had its own home-grown film star, Dorothy Mackaill, who rose from the Ziegfeld Follies chorus line to play opposite Clark Gable in No Man of Her Own (1932). Ian Carmichael is another Hull-born actor to have achieved success on the silver screen.

The Second World War and Postwar Period

The dramatic scene at Costello's Corner, Jameson Street, following an air raid in 1941. Miraculously, the statue of Andrew Marvell, poet and Hull's MP during the seventeenth-century Commonwealth, stands unscathed.

Surrounded by devastation, the statue of Queen Victoria, on the left, also escaped without damage. As one of Britain's main ports, Hull was a major target for the Luftwaffe during the Second World War. The city endured 82 air raids during which a total of 1,200 men, women and children were killed and 3,000 more seriously injured.

This is what was left of Bean Street after an attack in 1942. In its concern to maintain public morale, the government-controlled wartime media referred only to 'a north-east coast town' when reporting the appalling carnage in Hull. Other English towns and cities which suffered less were mentioned by name.

When the air raids finally ceased in April 1942, almost 87,000 houses in Hull had suffered structural damage; 152,000 people had been made homeless. Half the central area shops became rubble; one eighth of the total factory floor space and major stretches of dockland installations were destroyed. (A curious detail in this photograph is the white-gloved policeman at the foot of the statue who appears to have detected some serious cycling misdemeanour.)

'Britain Can Take It' was the defiant boast of the Blitz years – provided there was a nice cup of tea to follow, preferably accompanied by a 'fag'. In this instance, the tea is supplied by a member of the Women's Voluntary Service.

For the duration of the war, the gilded statue of William III was removed to the safety of the village of Sancton near Market Weighton, and only restored to its original site in the Market Place in 1948. The company that received the commission to remove the statue is still in business although it has updated its role as 'Machinery Merchant', displayed on the tailboard here, to become one of Hull's major suppliers of high-tech industrial air compressors.

A tranquil scene on the River Hull. The small ferry boat here crossed the river at the appropriately named Stoneferry. Ferry Lane Bridge now crosses the river at this point.

A few horses get
a wash and brush
up at the Horse
Wash near Victoria
Pier. Nearby, the
Rosalie Stamp
offloads its cargo.
It's difficult to see
what the cargo
actually is but
the van drawn up
alongside belongs
to Pullan & Ward,
'Wholesale Grocers,
Confectioners and
Yeast Merchants'.

This side-show
at the Hull Fair
in the 1950s
promises a
'Zoological
Sensation'
– '200 Monkeys
To Amuse and
Interest You'.
'How Human'
reads the placard
on the left
– 'Mother Monkey
and her Baby Boy'.
The 6d entrance
fee included
entertainment by
a 6-member brass
band.

67

The crew of the CW Jordan, built in 1907. Crew members participated in the profits from their catch and, although the captain took the largest share, trawlermen enjoyed the possibility of substantial rewards from a heavy catch – especially if they arrived at their home harbour well before their competitors.

St Andrew's fish dock, 1949. Note the Hull emblem of three crowns on the bow of the Kingston Jade. Hull's fishing trade boomed during the late 1940s and early '50s. 'As quickly as their catch can be brought up from the hold – tubs of plaice, turbot, halibut, codfish, ling, hake or herring – it is sold at auction to the fish buyers who attend from all the large towns of the north of England; and as quickly it is packed on board the waiting "Fish Trains" which will distribute it among the fifteen million people who live within the reach of the port of Hull.'

By the 1950s, male 'gippers' had replaced the fisher–girls of the earlier part of the century. But their employment would soon be threatened. In 1958, Iceland unilaterally declared a 12-mile fishing limit around its shores, a move which portended the Cod Wars of the '70s and the eventual collapse of Hull's fishing industry.

Shipbuilding and refitting continued to provide work in Hull, but this industry was also in terminal decline. The operation shown in the picture is technically known as reaming – widening or deepening a hole in the metal.

An elegant visitor to Hull in 1957 was the 3-master Pequod, the ship used in the filming of John Huston's Moby Dick, starring Gregory Peck. The fish meal factory in the background made this part of St Andrew's Dock extremely malodorous on hot summer days.

A young girl watches the Joseph Conrad steam into St Andrew's Dock, perhaps looking out for her trawlerman father on board. The Joseph Conrad was operated by the Newington Steam Trawling Company, which named all its vessels after authors with maritime connections. Built at Beverley in 1949, the trawler was scrapped in 1980.

A familiar sight during the 1940s and '50s, the Northern Dairies Commer lorries travelled the countryside collecting milk churns from the many small farms and bringing them back to the Northern Dairies depot. The company had been established in Hull in 1880 as a butter-importing business, but by the late '50s its operations stretched from Middlesbrough to Northampton, and westwards to North Wales and Northern Ireland. It is now part of Northern Foods.

One of Charles Batte's potato lorries offloading at the company's distribution centre in Humber Street.

The Humber Street market, 1952. This was Hull's wholesale fruit, flower and vegetable market and such was the volume of traffic that the street had already been made a one-way thoroughfare.

Lowgate in the 1950s, with the brewer's dray on the left showing that horse-drawn traffic hadn't completely disappeared. The church is St Mary's, originally built by the Knights Templar of North Ferriby in about 1327. The present building has a medieval nave and chancel but the main tower dates from 1697. The open arch at the base of the tower was created when Lowgate was widened in 1861. Two years later, the church was extensively altered by Giles Gilbert Scott during restoration work.

The Tivoli Theatre, 1947. The theatre was built on the corner of Paragon Street and South Street in 1871 as the New Theatre Royal. After the war, the Tivoli tried to attract custom by putting on titillating shows such as Piccadilly Peepshow. They were not successful. The theatre finally closed in 1954 and was demolished soon afterwards. The Hull Tax Office now occupies the site.

A jolly novel idea for a holiday. Specially converted carriages of the London North Eastern Railway were shunted on to quiet sidings or located at redundant stations to provide an unusual setting for a vacation. This one was sited in the Yorkshire Wolds near Wetwang.

'Delmo, the X-Ray Mind'. This particular variety of street entertainment was clearly very popular. Delmo, wearing what looks like some kind of academic gown, advertises himself with a puff from the Leicester Mail: 'The Blindfold Wonder Man of the X-Ray Mind'. Attracting much less custom is the stall, top left, apparently devoted entirely to a male grooming product. Shavol.

The early articulated lorries had a nasty habit of jack-knifing, which is clearly what has happened to this Foden vehicle operated by the nationalised freight carrier, British Road Services. The accident occurred on Boothferry Road on 27 February 1951. A splendidly attired AA officer appears to have taken control of the scene, while the policewoman in the background directs traffic around the accident.

A tobacconist's shop on Beverley Road in the late 1940s, a time when cigarette consumption was at its peak. It would be another few years before a scientific survey published in 1953 claimed that it had confirmed the link between smoking and lung cancer.

Hull Co-operative Society's travelling grocery service took to the roads in September 1953, providing a useful service for rural communities. Even then, small villages were poorly served by bus companies and only the most affluent rural residents could afford a car. As car ownership increased, this useful service became less necessary and it was phased out in the late '60s.

In November 1953 the River Hull burst its banks, flooding the Oxford Street neighbourhood near Wilcolmlee. These residents of Eleanor's Terrace seem to be quite enjoying the inundation. Flooding was a regular hazard until the Tidal Surge Barrier was erected in 1980.

Almost exactly a year later, a massive high tide caused serious flooding in the Witham area. This shopkeeper has barricaded the lower part of the door with board and rolled her trousers up to keep them dry. She appears to be standing on something unsteady which explains the supporting arm. The shop displays some vintage advertisements – for Walls banana flavour ice cream, Airman cigarettes and Anglo chewing gum among others.

The vicious winter of 1947–48 was so severe that ice floes appeared on the Humber, as seen in this photograph taken at Hessle Haven. In the city itself, the waters in the Railway Dock froze over completely, trapping more than a dozen vessels.

A peaceful scene on the outskirts of the city, 1950s. The skyline to the left is now dominated by the Humber Bridge.

The Swinging '60s
and into the '70s

Two young fans, Anne and Simon Escreet, met the Fab Four backstage at Hull's ABC cinema when the group performed there in October 1963. The Beatles returned to the city again in November 1964 when 'Beatlemania' was at its most frenzied. Ecstatically vocal teenage fans ensured that very little of the Beatles' singing could actually be heard.

The Beatles had taken the pop world by storm and they inspired countless imitators. This unidentified band, dressed in dazzling Lurex suits, was playing at the Skyline Ballroom on the top floor of the Co-operative building in Jameson Street.

The Skyline Ballroom also hosted the area semi-final of the World Disco Dancing Championships in 1968. Paradoxically, the '60s were the years when the BBC TV programme Come Dancing, featuring old-time dancing and shown in peak time, was at its most popular, attracting up to 12 million viewers.

Even more popular than Come Dancing was the Miss World competition. Not to be outdone, Hull ran its own beauty competition. These glamorous young ladies are competing for the title 'Miss Hull' in August 1972. From left to right they are Brenda Black, Gillian Clayton, Margaret Chapman, Patricia Holland, Karen Hope, Karen Martin, Josephine Sinclair, Barbara Woodhouse and Lynn Woodmansey.

The long hair and casual clothes of these 'beatniks', photographed in Queen's Gardens, would no doubt have outraged their parents who had endured the austerities and rigid moral code of the wartime years. The 'Beat Movement' had originated in California with Jack Kerouac's On The Road, which mocked the middle-class values of the 'tranquillised 50s'.

As fans arrive at Paragon station for the match between Hull City and Manchester United in August 1974, they are frisked by police. Violence and drunkenness on the terraces was already seen as a major public order issue. Later years were to witness much more serious disturbances.

Hull Gaol on Hedon Road. The stately old building shown earlier in this book is now protected by a formidable outer wall. The additional security was considered necessary after a number of serious disturbances in the gaol.

A common enough sight in the '60s, but two policewomen patrolling the Old City at night on foot wouldn't be countenanced nowadays. It was during the '60s that the police force began taking to their cars – the famous Z Cars immortalised in the BBC TV series of that name.

The first traffic wardens in Britain began patrolling the streets of London in 1961 but didn't reach Hull until 1966. The two wardens shown here were photographed as they set off on their first search for the city's parking malefactors.

A smiling traffic warden adds another ticket to the array already cluttering the windscreen of this illegally parked car. According to the Hull Daily Mail, the negligent owner had accumulated 42 tickets before he finally moved his vehicle.

For a few years, traffic wardens were also employed in directing traffic at busy junctions but the proliferation of traffic lights throughout the decade soon relieved them of this particular duty. Clearly, no great expense was incurred in the construction of the makeshift contraption in which this warden is standing.

What exactly was going on in Mayfield Street when this photograph was taken in 1974 isn't clear. The policeman in the background and the man holding an unreadable placard suggest that it's some kind of local protest, possibly in favour of 'traffic-calming measures', although that term hadn't yet entered the language. If you know the story behind this picture, please let me know.

A labour-intensive operation under way as council workmen, protected only by a line of oil lamps, paint road markings at the Fiveways roundabout on Boothferry Road. The church in the background is St Joseph's Catholic Church.

A bird's-eye view of the city in 1970 reveals some striking differences from the aerial shot taken in the 1920s and reproduced earlier in this book. The Queen's Gardens, created in 1935, can be seen centre left. The three docks forming a T-shape are Prince's Dock (now partly covered by the Prince's Dock Shopping Centre); the Humber Dock (now the Hull Marina); while the shaft of the T is formed by the Railway Dock, which is still functioning.

Despite extensive postwar redevelopment, the old city still had a large stock of sub-standard housing like this dead-end alley off Arundel Street. During the 1960s and '70s, the city made a determined effort to improve conditions. Swathes of Victorian, cheaply built terraces fell to the wrecker's ball and the dislodged residents were provided with new accommodation in . . .

. . . soulless high rise buildings like these tower blocks on Anlaby Road, constructed in 1965. This kind of high-density housing has since been soundly discredited, but at the time it met a crying need for new homes.

The final curtain is about to drop on the splendid Criterion Cinema. It was built in 1915 as the Majestic Cinema, enjoyed great success in the 1920s when it had its own resident orchestra to provide musical accompaniment to silent films, and finally closed in 1969. The demolition gang seen here began their work in 1973.

A scene guaranteed to give a present day Health and Safety Officer severe conniptions. The demolition worker giving a cheery wave isn't even wearing a safety helmet. The year was 1973; the location Mytongate.

Also in Mytongate, the following year, another building comes tumbling down. The tower covered in scaffolding in the background belongs to Holy Trinity Church. (A quarter of a century later, in June 2000, the tower was once again smothered by scaffolding.)

It seems odd that the derelict nurse's residence in the foreground was left standing while the spanking new Hull Royal Infirmary in the background was completed. The Infirmary stands on the site of a Georgian hospital of 1782 which when it was built stood in open countryside outside the town.

The Hull Royal Infirmary was opened by Queen Elizabeth in June 1967. She arrived accompanied by the Lord Lieutenant of East Yorkshire, Lord Middleton, on the left. To the right stands a 'guard of honour' of white-gloved nurses, representatives of the 700 staff who would be employed in serving the new hospital.

It's November 1962 and these children in Ferensway have taken advantage of new technology to capture the attention of passers-by. 'George, the Speaking Guy' has been equipped with one of the new-fangled portable tape recorders, and programmed to transmit the traditional appeal of 'A Penny for the Guy'.

Another of the city's new buildings was the Hull & East Riding Co-operative Society's department store on Jameson Street. The store is now occupied by BHS but the huge mural celebrating Hull's maritime heritage is still in place. The city seems to have a fondness for murals. Two more are featured later in this book and among others is a colourful creation marking the UN Year of the Disabled, 1981, which can be seen by visitors to Hull's Central Library.

An atmospheric scene at the Jameson Street fountain in the days just before Christmas 1962. For the child on the left, protectively encircled by her mother's arms, this must surely have been a magical moment.

This grocer's shop on Eastbourne Street offered its customers a strange mix. The counter in the foreground displays a selection of hygienically unprotected home-made pies and snacks. In contrast, behind the state-of-the-art bacon slicer, the back shelves are stacked with products dedicated to zapping every kind of laundry problem.

After years of agonised public debate, legislation permitting betting shops to operate was finally passed in 1960. This 'Turf Accountant's Office' in Hull opened on the first day they became legal – 1 May 1961.

The Lincoln Castle ferry boat approaches the Victoria Pier. During its years in service, the Lincoln Castle made 226,000 crossings and carried 23 million passengers. Despite her shallow draught, only 4ft 6in, she often managed to run aground on the Humber sandbanks.

E-type Jaguars destined for export are lined up on King George's Dock in the summer of 1963. First produced in 1961, the E-types set a standard of elegance for sports cars that in the opinion of many has never been equalled. They continued in production until 1975. In the serried ranks of cars on the dockside are some of the popular Mini-Coopers which also first appeared in 1961. Both models made considerable contributions to Britain's desperately needed export sales at this time.

Another trawler named after a popular author. The H180 Hammond Innes was built at Beverley in 1972 and was one of the last trawlers to be completed before the demise of the Hull fishing fleet following the Cod Wars. It was the winner of the Silver Cod Trophy for the trawler making the greatest haul of cod in a single year. The diesel-engined vessel, 191ft long and with a beam of 37.1ft, was manned by a crew of fifteen.

The '70s was a decade of industrial unrest all around the country and especially in the docks. There were numerous strikes and serious disruption of traffic in the port. Hull had been something of a pioneer in Trade Union history: as one of the banners in this photograph proclaims, it was way back in 1791 that Hull workers formed the first British Co-operative.

A rather more stately procession of senior officials of Hull University, 1962. Too lowly in the university hierarchy to have taken part in this ceremonial event was Philip Larkin, the celebrated poet who was the university's librarian from 1955 until 1983.

Built at Beverley in 1960, the Arctic Corsair was one of the last of the 'sidewinders' – trawlers which hauled in their catch over the side of the vessel rather than at the stern. When it was taken out of service, it was converted into a museum of the trawling industry.

The Old City's High Street runs parallel to the River Hull, and in Georgian times it was lined with the substantial houses of shipowners who could keep an eye on their vessels from their drawing-rooms. One such entrepreneur was Robert Wilberforce, father of William, the great campaigner against slavery. Almost three centuries later, as this photograph taken in 1962 shows, residential housing and shipping still coexisted at close quarters.

A thickly gloved officer of the Port of Hull Authority removes two of the less acceptable catches from a trawler in the 1960s. Canal boats suffered even more from these pests. In A Life on the Humber, Harry Fletcher remembers that 'We spent a lot of our time catapulting at rats under the landing-stages. They were the biggest I have ever seen, as big as large cats, and at night when we were in bed we could hear them running about the decks.'

99

The interior of St Barnabas's Church, decorated with maritime artefacts for the annual Harvest of the Sea Festival. The church's dedication to St Barnabas reflects his standing as the patron saint of fishermen.

Back in 1965, the Hull Agricultural Show considered it natural to invite the local Hunt to take part in its showcase of local activities and interests. By the late 1980s, however, the hostility of animal welfare groups opposed to hunting by hounds had made such displays problematic. They were quietly excluded from the Show's programme of events.

Modern Hull

Opened by the Queen in July 1981, the Humber Bridge is still the longest single span suspension bridge in the world, its main span stretching for 4,626 ft (1,410 metres). It's an awesome construction but as a major roadway it leads nowhere. The A15 road south of the bridge peters out into a perpetually congested single lane highway.

Labour's Transport Secretary Bill Rodgers visited the work in progress in 1977. It was his predecessor as Transport Secretary, Barbara Castle, who had promised the people of Humberside that they would get their bridge, dismissing predictions that it would be a costly white elephant.

The staggering quantity of materials required for the bridge's construction included 44,000 miles of cable wire, 27,065 tons of steel and 472,417 tons of concrete.

Painters at work on the Humber Bridge, not a job for anyone who suffers from vertigo. The two concrete towers soar 500ft (155 metres) and the carriageway floats 98ft (30 metres) above high water level.

The ferry boat Lincoln Castle, in BR livery, on one of its last journeys before the bridge opened. After being taken out of service, the vessel was bought by the Waterfront Hotel Club and for more than a decade served as a restaurant and museum located at the foot of the bridge which had made her redundant.

The launching of the Hoo Crest, 1986. Like the fishing industry, shipbuilding had suffered an almost total collapse in the last quarter of the century. Only occasionally could the shipyards make a splash like this.

The Queen Elizabeth Dock container terminal, 1989. The latter part of the twentieth century saw a steady growth in traffic through the port. Hull is still Britain's leading port for timber, and more than 10 million tonnes of freight is handled here each year.

The ill-fated Gaul, which sank off the coast of Norway under mysterious circumstances in February 1974 with the loss of 36 lives. A formal investigation in 1999 confirmed the original finding that the trawler had sunk after being pummelled by 40ft waves. But the families of the dead sailors remain convinced that the Gaul was structurally unsound.

After standing warning at the tip of Spurn Point for 50 years, the Spurn Lightship is now permanently moored in the Hull Marina, converted into a museum. Visitors are welcome to step on board and discover how the lightship operated. The striking sculpture in the foreground is titled Cormorant Boat. Created by Kate Hartford, it was the winner of the 1986/7 Hull Open Sculpture Competition.

As the city approached the third millennium, evidence was discovered of maritime activity in the area in prehistoric times. In 1986, this prehistoric log boat was discovered at Hasholme. It was taken to the Beverley Road Baths for a wash and brush up.

Bingo was at the height of its popularity in the 1980s. This caller's striking tie has an interesting design based on snowflakes and was very much in keeping with the vogue of the time for 'kipper' ties.

Eyes Down at one of the city's largest bingo halls, 1984. At top right of the photograph, hanging from the ceiling, can be seen some of the prizes on offer.

Entertainment al fresco in Jameson Street, 1989. The versatile busker, Les Prentice, includes guitar, mouth organ and drums among his instruments, while his performing pooch adds a touch of canine ballet.

Much more energetic entertainment was provided at the Hull City Hall Ballroom Dancing Competition,
November 1986. Around this time, ballroom dancers were making an impassioned plea to be recognised as an
Olympic sport, an ambition they have not yet realised.

Football continued to be the most popular spectator sport. Captain Roger Millward is chaired by his Kingston Rovers team-mates after their victory against Hull in 1980.

In Victoria Square, Roger Millward displays the Express Challenge Cup to the team's jubilant fans.

In June 1986, workmen installed this rather glum-looking statue in a quiet corner of Queen's Gardens. It's named Mankind under Threat and was sculpted in bronze by Jimmy Boyle, a reformed convicted murderer. The statue was unveiled by local playwright Alan Plater.

Costing £15,000, the statue was a gift to the city from Northern Foods whose chairman at the time, Alec Horsley, was involved in schemes to assist ex-prisoners. It looks across the gardens to the Wilberforce Monument and the Hull College of Further Education.

In 1986, a small development of houses was built off Selby Road. The architect had the bright idea of livening up the blank end walls by using darker-coloured bricks to create various images. One of them is a railway train; this one appears to suggest a rugby tackle.

Hull's tradition of creating large public murals was continued in 1993 when this dramatic depiction of the city's maritime heritage was painted. Named the Spirit of Hessle Road, it includes examples of the various types of vessel to have used the port and characters associated with the area.

Even bingo couldn't save this grand old cinema. The flamboyant Eureka Picture Palace on Hessle Road closed as a cinema in 1977 and for several years survived as a bingo hall. Plans are under way to redevelop this area of Hessle Road, but whether this splendid frontage will be retained is not yet known.

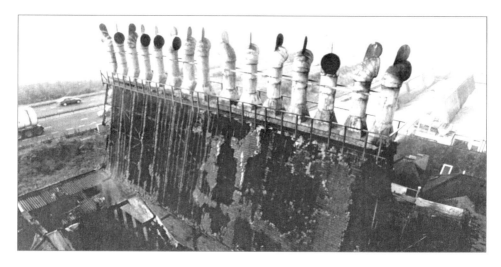

Elsewhere, regeneration of the city continued throughout the 1990s. This fish smoking house used to stand in West Dock Street before being demolished in 1994.

Despite the devastating air raids of the Second World War, a surprising number of Hull's ancient buildings survived. This is the Old Grammar School, founded by Bishop Alcock of Ely in 1486. Its most famous pupils are Andrew Marvell and William Wilberforce, both of whom became MPs for the town. Andrew Marvell, whose statue now stands in front of the school, was the first of a succession of distinguished Hull-born poets that includes Stevie Smith, Philip Larkin and the present Poet Laureate, Andrew Motion. The school is now a museum with collections dedicated to Victorian Britain and the history of Hull and its people.

Across the square from the Grammar School is Trinity House (1753), which was established to give 'such effectual instructions to poor boys, as may nurse them for the sea service'. It still does, although it now also admits girls. The steel sculpture to the left of the picture records in a circular scroll crucial episodes in the history of the city, beginning with its charter, granted in 1299, through the plague of 1478 and the city's defiance of Charles I, and concluding with the city's 700th birthday in 1999.

The old and the new are combined in this striking photograph. In the foreground is the gilded equestrian statue of William III, erected in 1734; in the background stands the guillotine-shaped structure of the Tidal Surge Barrier at the mouth of the River Hull. The barrier was built in 1980 at a cost of £54 million to protect the Old Town against flooding during unusually high tides. Operated for the first time in August of that year, when a higher than normal tide was predicted, the barrier worked perfectly.

Throughout the 1990s, what were once run-down dockside areas were completely transformed. Imaginative redevelopment has created a totally different environment, enticing visitors with a wide range of dockside pubs, restaurants, cafés, clubs and attractive waterside walks.

In 1991, the former Prince's Dock became the Prince's Quay Shopping Centre. It stands on 500 massive concrete stilts above the historic dock and was completed at a total cost of £65 million.

The Centre's 70 different stores, on 4 levels, offers one of the best 'shop-till-you-drop' experiences in the north-east. The spacious ground-floor atrium also provides an unusual venue for performances of various kinds. On this occasion, a full 40-member orchestra is entertaining the shoppers.

Prominent among many impressive modern buildings in the city is the Crown Court complex on Alfred Gelder Street. Those brought here to face criminal charges may not be particularly interested in its architectural merits, but it's a curious fact that the Home Office has an impressive record of commissioning well-designed complexes such as this all around the country.

A mantle of snow covers Queen's Gardens in the heart of the city. In the background rises the triple-towered outline of the former Hull Docks Office, now the city's Maritime Museum. It was built more than a century ago when Victorian self-confidence was at its peak. Closing the book on a tumultuous twentieth century, the city enters the twenty-first once again displaying the same kind of energy and initiative that inspired its Victorian forebears.

Back in 1299 the city was granted a charter to hold an autumn fair. It began as a fairly modest cattle and sheep mart but over the centuries it expanded into the largest gathering of its kind in Europe. Held in October, Hull Fair is now a 9-day extravaganza occupying a 14-acre site crammed with every imaginable variety of entertainment.

Acknowledgements
and Picture Credits

Most of the photographs from the first half of the twentieth century reproduced in this book have been selected from Ken Jackson's photographic collection at his 'Memory Lane' shop on Hessle Road, Hull. This book includes more than a hundred of his pictures – a tiny proportion of the 10,000 images of Humberside that Ken has amassed over the years.

More recent photographs have been supplied by the Hull Daily Mail's helpful librarian Anne Brittain (p. 80 lower, p. 81 both, p. 82 both, p. 84 both, p. 85, p. 92, p. 94 lower, p. 107, p. 108 both, p. 109), and by Innes Photographers, Hessle (p. 69, p. 75 lower,p. 76 lower, p. 77 both, p. 78, p. 80 upper, p. 91 lower, p. 95 lower). I would also like to thank the staff of the Local History Department of Hull Central Library for their unfailingly courteous response to endlessly bothersome enquiries; to Stephen Betts for the loan of photographs from his personal collection (p. 22 upper, p. 27 upper, p. 53 lower); Hull City Council (p. 101, p. 111 lower, p. 115 lower, p. 116 both, p. 117, p. 118,p. 119); and to Patrick Howlett (p. 50 lower, p. 78 upper, p. 100 lower, p. 102 lower, p. 120). I am also deeply indebted to Ken Jackson (who kindly lent me the photographs that form the endpapers to this book) and Patrick Howlett who shared their lifelong knowledge of the area and helped me in identifying the various photographs. Any errors that remain are my own.